HEROIC STORIES from the Book of Mormon

By SHAUNA GIBBY
Illustrated by CASEY NELSON

DESERET BOOK

Salt Lake City, Utah

© 2017 Shauna N. Gibby

Illustrations © 2017 Casey Nelson

All rights reserved. No part of this book may be reproduced in any form or by any means without permission in writing from the publisher, Deseret Book Company, at permissions@deseretbook.com or P. O. Box 30178, Salt Lake City, Utah 84130. This work is not an official publication of The Church of Jesus Christ of Latter-day Saints. The views expressed herein are the responsibility of the author and do not necessarily represent the position of the Church or of Deseret Book Company.

Deseret Book is a registered trademark of Deseret Book Company.

Visit us at DeseretBook.com

Library of Congress Cataloging-in-Publication Data

(CIP data on file)
ISBN 978-1-62972-319-8

Printed in China
RR Donnelley, Shenzhen, Guangdong, China   3/2017

10 9 8 7 6 5 4 3 2 1

*To two of my greatest heroes,
John and Russell.*

—SG

*To my friends and family.
I love you up to the moon, all day.*

—CN

There are many wonderful heroes in the Book of Mormon. We can learn from their examples. If you look closely at each page, you will discover some fun facts about these great people.

Shine a flashlight behind the color pages to see what is hidden in each Book of Mormon scene.

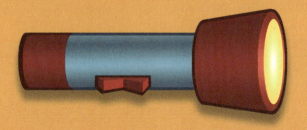

Lehi was a prophet in Jerusalem a long time ago. He saw many visions from the Lord.

What important event did he see?

Lehi saw that Jesus Christ would be born and become the Savior of the world.

Lehi taught his family about the things he saw.

Nephi made tools.

The Lord showed him where to find the metal and how to make the tools he needed to build the ship.

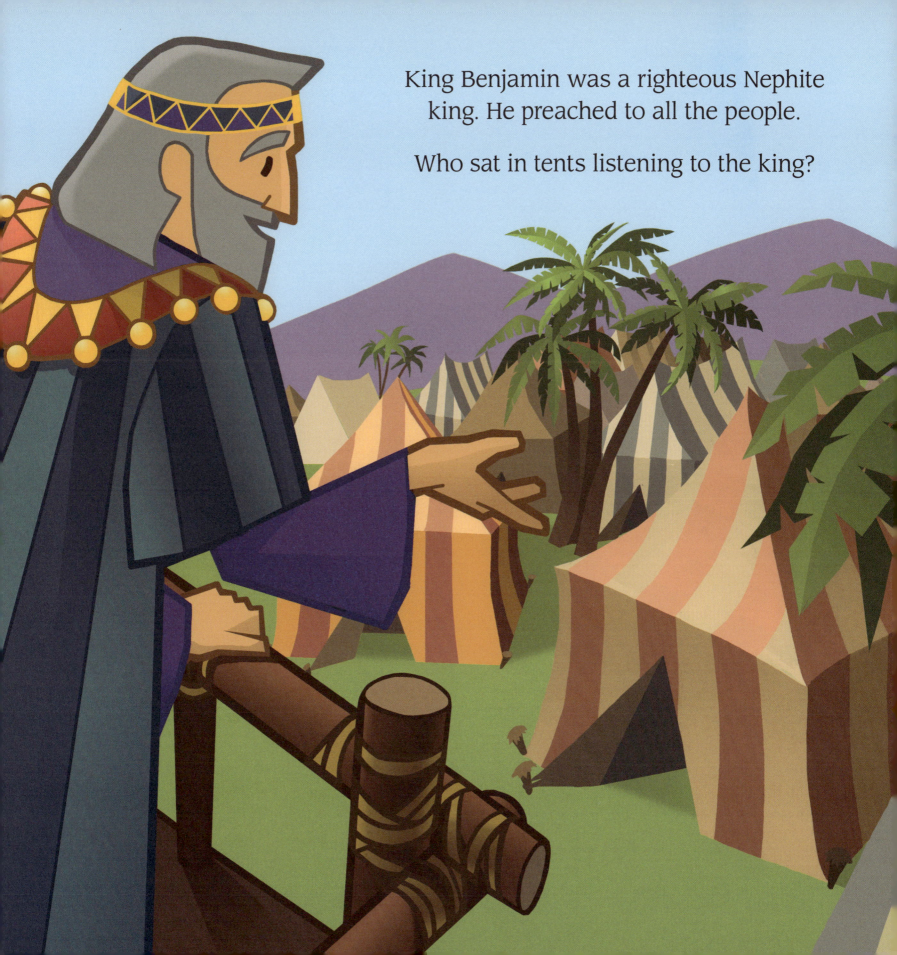

Families!

Many families pitched their tents facing the king so they could hear his important message. He taught them to serve one another.

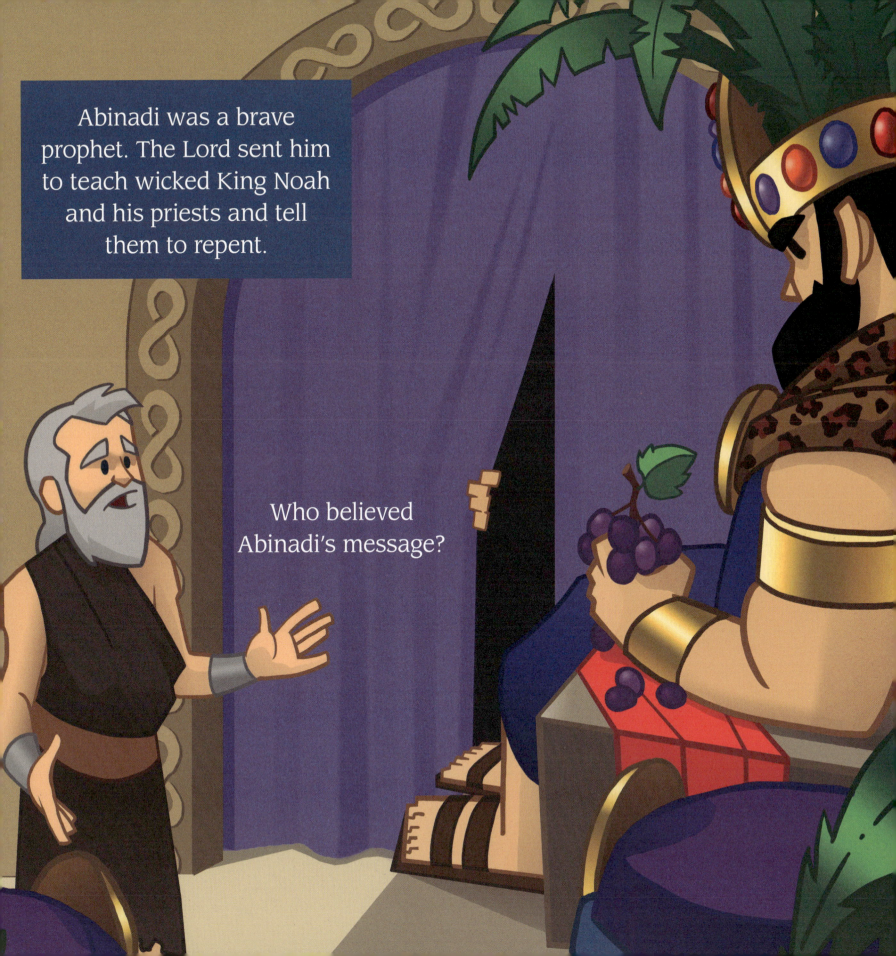

Alma was one of the king's priests. He was the only one who believed the truths that Abinadi taught.

Alma escaped from King Noah's court and taught many people the words he heard from Abinadi about Jesus Christ. What did the people do when they heard?

They chose to be baptized and become members of the Lord's church.

Alma's son was also named Alma. After Alma the Younger was converted to the gospel, he spent his whole life teaching about Christ. He taught the people that having faith is like planting a seed.

What will happen to the seed after it is planted?

If the seed is cared for, it will grow into a **large tree**.

Faith also grows as a person wants to believe and does what is right.

Ammon was a wonderful missionary. He taught and converted many Lamanites.

What could he have chosen to be instead?

A king! Ammon's father was King Mosiah. Ammon could have been the next king, but he chose to be a missionary.

Abish had a testimony of Jesus Christ and His gospel. She told all the Lamanites in her city to come see something important. What was it?

After hearing Ammon teach, the Lamanite king and queen were overcome by the Spirit and fell unconscious. Abish wanted everyone to see and to know the truth of the gospel. Soon the king awoke and encouraged everyone to learn about Jesus.

Captain Moroni was a great Nephite leader. He made something important.

What was it?

Captain Moroni made a flag out of his coat, called the title of liberty, to help the people remember to defend their families, faith, and freedom.

Helaman was a prophet and a soldier in the Nephite army.

Who chose Helaman to be their leader?

More than two thousand young Lamanite warriors wanted Helaman to lead them into battle. Although they had never fought before, they were not afraid. They helped to save their people, and the Lord protected them so that none of them were killed.

Samuel stood high on the city wall to preach to the people. He told the Nephites to repent. When the people tried to kill him with rocks and arrows, God protected Samuel.

The brother of Jared was the leader of the Jaredites. God led them to the seashore, where they built boats. They needed light inside their boats. How were they able to see in the darkness?

The brother of Jared melted sixteen **clear stones** out of rock. The Lord answered his prayer and touched the stones so they would glow. Then the Jaredites had lights for their boats.

A prophet named Mormon gathered the writings of past prophets and put them together onto golden plates. Who was he making this record for?

Mormon was inspired to know that someday people would read this book and learn about Jesus Christ. He wanted us to have the blessings of the gospel.

Mormon's son Moroni finished the book his father had created.

Where did he put the golden plates?

Moroni buried the plates in a stone box and covered it with a large rock. The Lord told him where to put them so they would be safe until they could be translated by Joseph Smith many years later.

The Book of Mormon contains Heavenly Father's plan for His people. We can learn many things when we read it.

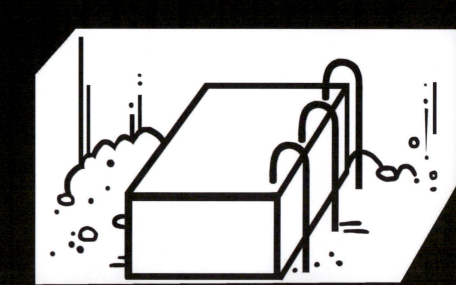